THE I LOVE TO Fart COOKBOOK

THE I LOVE TO Fart COOKBOOK

Travis W. Pacone

DOUBLE EAGLE
Press

ISBN: 0-943084-04-0

First printing May 1983

Manufactured in the United States of America

Published by

DOUBLE EAGLE, INC.
1124 N. Derbyshire
Arlington Hts., IL 60004

This book is dedicated to:

Mike Potishnak, the Guru of the Gastrointestinal System and a good friend.

ORIGINAL PROTOTYPE MODEL
OF FLUFF-O-METER

Shown here, the first working model of the Fluff-O-Meter. Designed and built in 1927 by Dr. Travis W. Pacone, Sr., after 20 years of research. As advanced as this machine was for its time, it was limited to the simple rating of flatulence tone.

Ruins of the original prototype can be seen on permanent exhibit in the PACONE OFFICIAL MUSEUM OF FART STUDIES (POOFS). This ingenious bit of machinery was unfortunately destroyed in 1954 during an analysis of the effects of recipe #7 (Swamp Gas Soup). Later models have incorporated various "overload" circuits making it possible to study further advances in Fartology.

NEW ADVANCED MODEL
DIGITAL FLUFF-O-METER

Using modern technology, the new improved digital Fluff-O-Meter differs from the crude prototype in its ability to rate speed, power and aroma as well as tone. This model of modern technology also features digital read out, making scientific study more accurate.

With overload circuits, this model can handle all but the most exotic farts which still tend to cause meltdown and raise the possibility of the China Syndrome. (educated professionals know the real reason behind the Three Mile Island disaster)

Treasure of Sierra Madre

2 tablespoons vegetable oil	20 oz. of cooked or canned tomatoes
4 tablespoons toasted wheat germ	1 tablespoon chili powder
1 pound ground beef	2 cups canned kidney beans
1½ teaspoons salt	3 pinches paprika
½ cup tofu	½ cup boiling water

Heat oil in kettle. Add meat. Increase heat until meat browns. Add everything but beans and tofu. Cover and cook at low heat for 45 min. Add beans and tofu and cook for 30 min.

8.8 on the meter. Watch out, your sphincter may sue for separate maintenance.

The Winds of Wheat Germ
apologies to Herman Wouk

1 (10 oz.) package of frozen broccoli	½ teaspoon of salt
1¼ cups of milk	½ teaspoon of nutmeg
3 eggs beaten lightly	½ cup of grated cheese
1 teaspoon of wheat germ	

Preheat oven to 350°. Cook broccoli in boiling water for 3 minutes; drain. Pour milk into sauce pan. Boil and let cool till lukewarm. Mix eggs with salt, wheat germ, and nutmeg. Add milk and cheese, beating constantly. Pour into greased baking dish. Add the broccoli.

Bake 30 to 40 minutes or until knife inserted into the center comes out clean. Serve hot.

The Fluff-o-Meter doesn't measure odor, so it only registers a 7. Silent but deadly indeed!

Favorite recipe of World War II submariners. Lack of sound would keep them safe from enemy destroyer's sonar detectors. Many a torpedo was fired this way. (Run silent, run deep)

Sometimes called "Depth-Charge Delights."

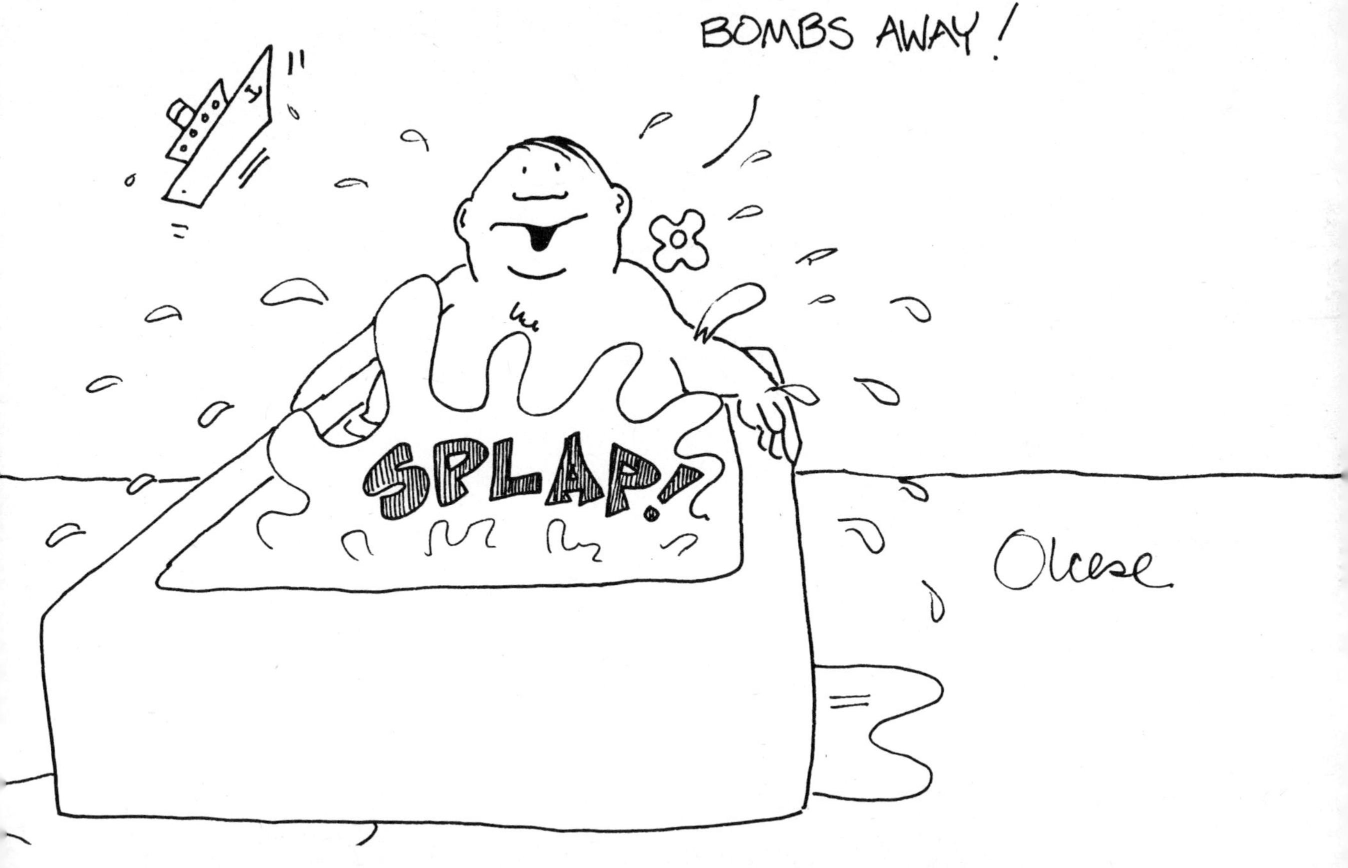
BOMBS AWAY!
SPLAP!
Olcese

Casablanca Gestapo Chaser

CHAMPAGNE COCKTAIL

(2 dashes of bitters on lump of sugar. Place sugar in champagne glass. Fill with cold champagne. Add twist of lemon.)

BEER CHASER (imported)

Champagne Cocktail and the beer chaser should be gulped.

A 4.4 on the Fluff-o-Meter. And you thought "Rick's" cleared out because Peter Lorre was being arrested. Now you know why they wouldn't let Rick on the plane at the end. ("It doesn't take much to see that the problems of 3 little people don't amount to a hill of beans in this crazy world.")

"You must remember this, a fart is still a fart". ·

Turkey Talkback Stuffing

2 tablespoons butter	1 cup wheat germ
1 tablespoon chopped onion	½ pound raisins
1 cup finely chopped celery stem and tops	grated ½ lemon rind
2 tablespoons chopped parsley	¼ teaspoon salt
1½ cups bread crumbs	

Cook onion, celery, and parsley in the butter for a few minutes. Mix
in the raisins with the crumbs and wheat germ. Stir in the cooked
vegetables. Add lemon rind and salt. STUFF IT!

This one could ruffle a few feathers. (Is that the mating call of the
Northern Goose or the ever resounding echo of a robustly roasted
turkey?)

Last Thanksgiving my house was surrounded by hundreds of horny
ganders. They held my down ski jacket hostage, demanding to be
allowed in. Talk about ugly ducklings!

An Air of Controversy

We were two days out of Katmandu and, as we hiked up the narrow trail, the Grand Himalayas came into view. Magnificent these greatest of all mountain ranges! Off in the distance I could see Everest and, as I reached the top of the hill I stood with my guides around me simply staring, paying homage to these grand peaks. My spirits soared! I was sure this would be the day. After months of searching the mountains and foothills of Nepal I felt finally, this would be the day.

Suddenly, breaking my entranced stare was Govinda tapping me on the shoulder. He pointed towards a distant ridge.

"Temple!", he shouted.

I turned. There it was. Just as the legends described. After all these years. And still intact. I signaled my guides to follow as I made my way down the hill towards the temple. Hesitantly, they followed.

I stood at the mouth of the temple. My heart raced with anticipation. The guides stood well behind me as I stared into the blackness of the entrance. It bore deeply into the hill in which the temple was built. I lit a torch and signaled for the guides to follow.

They stepped back and simply stared in terror at the black abyss. I signaled again, this time forcibly. But they slowly inched backwards and suddenly turned and ran. I shouted for them to return but to no avail. They were gone.

A strange musty air swept from this ancient temple causing my torch light to dance in a spastic glow. My palms were wet with sweat. I gripped the torch tightly and bravely made my way into the temple. I was instantly swallowed up by the blackness. Slowly I walked with the glow of my torch as my protecting aura. It threw a dim light upon the ancient tunnel walls. I stopped from time to time to brush away the dust which had accumulated over thousands of years. Suddenly, the tunnel ended. I raised my torch high, slowly sweeping it in front of me.

"An altar!", I gasped.

There before me, carved into the solid wall of rock it stood, the ancient etching of my quest: the God Paji Hawama Phutnu. My theory had been correct. He did exist!

The above is an excerpt from my diary which was the basis for my best selling book, "Cheese Cutting of the Gods".

In the Summer of 1953 I had tried to find evidence supporting my contention that the "God" Paji Hawama Phutnu (in Nepali meaning "bad airburst") was actually an alien who had traveled to this planet to teach

Earthlings the art of farting; an extra-terrestrial passing on of secrets to mankind.

Nepal was not only the only site where I have sought the origin and possible cosmic connection of the fart. My widely read and critically acclaimed, "Foul Caverns of Tunisia" sends shivers up and down one's nose as I describe the unmistakable odors emanating from those caves.

In South America, my aerial photographs of the Ridges of Rualfo show that, from the air and only from the air, those complex network of lines form the shape of a buttock.

Do these finds explain the mysterious mammoth bowl of golden beans that adorns the Aztec temple in Central America?

These and additional shocking finds have led me on the trail of baffling mysteries. In 1968 I searched for the Abominable Skunkman of the Hymalayas. In 1971 I contend I had found day old tracks of the legendary Big Fart of the American northwest. And I have recently announced plans for a future expedition to investigate bubbles sighted rising up from the depths of Loch Ness, Scotland.

My continuing tireless search for the origins and true meaning of the fart have taken me to the far corners of the Earth where I have found that endless myths and legends, like a mysterious cloud, obscure the facts.

This book is my attempt to clear the air, to dispel some of the myths while, at the same time, pass on some of the most interesting of my findings: a unique assortment of recipes which I have encountered in my travels.

— Travis W. Pacone

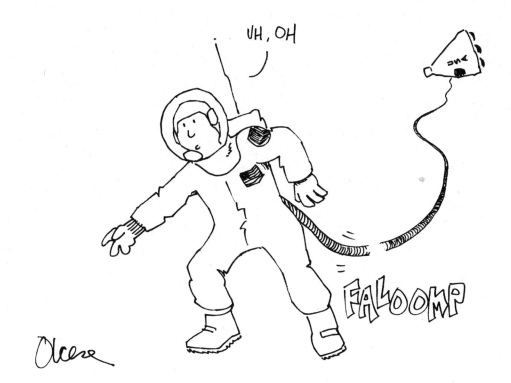

4.5

1 banana	1 scoop butter pecan ice cream
1 tablespoon chopped pecans	1 scoop butter almond ice cream
1 tablespoon chopped cashews	1 scoop vanilla ice cream
1 tablespoon coconut	whipped cream

Slice banana down the middle. Place 3 scoops inside of the halves.

Sprinkle on pecans, cashews, and coconut. Add whip cream.

4.5 on Fluffer. Watch out, this dish could melt your igloo. Make your very own Aurora Borealis. Eskimos use this one to keep polar bears away. (The call of the wild!)

Nacho chips

Raisins

Cashews

Apple juice

Snacking on the first three while gulping casually on the apple juice
will create a 5.1 on the Fluff Meter.

The name of the snack is a bit deceiving. It's more of a "cute" fart
than an earthquake. The kind that makes the Valley Girls titter. If this
dish catches on, Nevada will want to PUSH California into the Pacific.
("Gowdy Brad! Totally Awesome! Where'd you learn to do that!")

Tahitian Trade Wind Pudding

7.8

¼ cup shortening	1 teaspoon vanilla
¾ cup sugar	2 beaten egg whites
1 cup sifted flour	3 cups coconut shreds
¼ teaspoon salt	¼ cup raisins
1 teaspoon baking powder	¼ cup diced pineapple
¼ cup milk	

Cream the shortening and slowly add in the sugar. Stir in dry ingredients and add milk. Fold in beaten egg whites. Add vanilla. Mix in coconut. Place in the bottom of a greased pudding dish. Pour batter over coconut. Bake at 350°F, 1¼ hours. Add pineapple and raisins after baking is done.

Fluff says 7.8. This one could have been the real reason for the mutiny aboard the HMS Bounty.

Flatulence Etiquette

One of the great awakenings in my life was the fact that everybody farts. It took me quite a while to be comfortable with the fact that President Eisenhower, Joe DiMaggio and even Walter Cronkite farted. To me, flatulence was something you outgrew, like acne or picking your nose. No, we all fart and we always will.

I remember in high school all the boys boasted of wanting to marry a virgin. It was my wish to marry a girl who had never farted. This, of course, put a crimp in my social life. I did meet one girl, her name was Patty. Everything was teriffic until one day she exploded in Algebra class. It was a very traumatic experience for me. From that point on I had to face up to it: "it" being the universal truth that **everyone** farts. The problem now is, what to do about it?

A burp can have a simple "excuse me" erase the sin. However, "Excuse me" does not eradicate the lowly fart. What do you do then? Following are some ways to deal with the fart.

The Denial:

1. Turn to the person next to you and loudly blame them. (Be sure to draw the attention of others). Remind them how rude and disgusting they are. If they're the type that embarrasses easily, their reddened face will condemn them for sure.

If you are dealing with a truckdriver, professional wrestler, pituitary giant or any other large type person who might grind you into bean curd, be more subtle. Make an annoyed, disgusted expression, wave your hand in front of your nose (behind their back), glance at them again and quietly walk away shaking your head in annoyance.

Pet Blame:

1. Blame the dog, cat, cow, elephant, bus or canary. (i.e. "I guess I'll never be able to teach Fido any manners!")

2. Point skyward and yell, "Look! A flock of Canadian Geese!"

Subterfuge:

1. Pretend a car has just honked for you. Turn and call out. "OK, I'll be right out!"

2. The speed of a fart at sea level has been timed at 10.4 feet/second. If you can move quickly in the opposite direction ("For every action there is an equal and opposite reaction" — Newton.) you can escape "ground zero" and be gone by the time the deed has been detected. The "tail" dissipates as you move (so keep moving). This is known as the "Comet Effect".

3. As soon as you fart, grab your throat and fake a blocked air passage. When a couple of pats on the back are administered, you can revive. After the shock and commotion are over, no one will remember that you farted. (If your rescuer is attractive, you might want to hold out for mouth-to-mouth resuscitation).

4. Upon farting, suddenly start to shake and roll around on the floor screaming out that the ghost of Ivan the Terrible (a prodigious farter) has taken possession of your colon. Have someone run out to get an exorcist.

5. Tell them you're an orthodox Buddist (recipe: Methane Mantra).

Prevention:

1. Hold very still and think about baseball or sex.

2. Tighten up your anal muscle. This is an obvious method and may only postpone the inevitable. It may, however, give you the time to sneak off to privacy. (Caution: Abuse of this method may irritate your bacteria and can bring about anti-social behavior such as holding your pancreas hostage or doing a buck 'n wing on your appendix. And don't forget poor Patty of Algebra class fame!)

In Case of Silent but Deadly:

1. Explain to those nearby that the sewer has backed up.

2. Explain that you heard a truck carrying manure has just collided with a truck full of ripe cheese.

3. Have everyone present join in a rousing chorus of "God Bless America". (Breathing in and out of the mouth will prevent the nose from picking up odor).

4. Move in front of fan (not too close!). If no fan is available, wave hand.

5. Yell out, "Hey! That's not my brand!"

6. Use the aforementioned "Comet Effect".

7. Casually explain that it's getting rather stuffy and windows should be opened.

8. Blame it on the dog, cat, cow, elephant, bus or canary.

1.5

Whispering Winds Salad

½ cup apples (diced)

½ cup celery (diced)

¼ cup sunflower seeds

¼ cup coconut

Mix and munch.

For rookies. 1.5 on the Fluff-o-Meter. Good dish to break in virgin bacteria. (Be gentle, this is my first fart)

Roadrunner Salad

Serves 8

1 (16 oz.) can of cut green beans	¼ cup cider vinegar
1 (16 oz.) can of yellow or wax beans	2 cups sliced celery
1 (16 oz.) can of kidney beans	4 mint leaves
1 can apple sauce	

Drain beans. Heat apple sauce and vinegar. Mix in beans and celery and crush in mint leaves.

Records 6 on the Fluff-o-Meter. So this was the Roadrunner's secret! Poor old coyote. And you thought that was a cloud of dust the old bird was leaving behind. (BEEP! BEEP!)

Alabama Atom Smasher

Pecan pie

Rum raisin ice cream

Just cut a piece of the pie and top with ice cream.

Good ole boy Fluffer gives it a 5. Sometimes called GENERAL LEE'S REVENGE. With this dish, old times won't soon be forgotten. The Johnny Rebs used to sit around the campfire and toot "Dixie" after a few slices. (Not too close to the fire boys!)

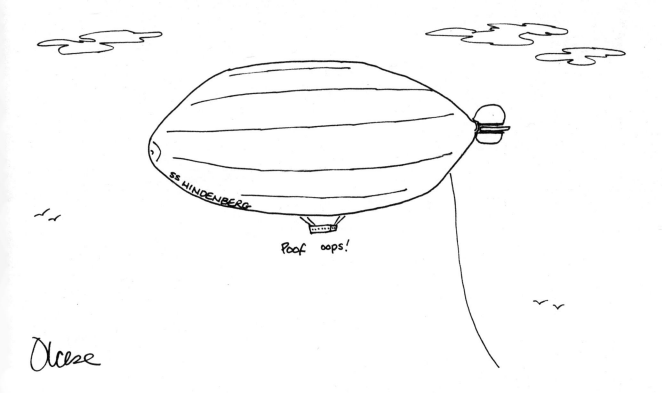

5

Rumble Seat Salad

¼ cup walnuts (diced)

¼ cup sunflower seeds

¼ cup raisins

¼ cup diced dried apples

Mix. Enjoy

Rates a 5. For the faint of heart. Weaker relative to BISON BLASTER.
Safer, but you'll never see "the rockets red glare."

Lentil Launcher

1 cup lentils

4 cups water

¼ cup chopped celery

2 tablespoons tomato paste

1 bay leaf

¼ teaspoon oregano

½ teaspoon salt

Soak lentils overnight in 1 cup of water. Mix ingredients. Cook for 2½ hours, 'til lentils are soft. Remove bay leaf.

Give it a 7. Won't kill any bison, but you may lose a few friends. If they can't take a joke . . .

1 (10 oz.) package frozen lima beans

¼ cup chopped onion

2 tablespoons margarine

1 cup canned tomatoes

½ teaspoon dried mint leaves

¼ cup diced celery

Cook beans according to the directions on the package. Set aside. In medium skillet saute onion and celery until tender. Stir in mint, beans and tomatoes; heat until piping hot. 4 servings.

Not spectacular, but smooth. A high class fart. You won't even have to excuse yourself. Rates a 6.

2 bananas

¼ cup honey

¼ cup raisins

¼ cup cashews or brazil nuts

4 tablespoons coconut

Mash up bananas well. Mix in honey. Mix in other ingredients.

Doesn't look pretty but if you want to honk with the geese, this is your baby. Your bacteria will give you a standing ovation. (Is that applause I hear?)

Fart Facts & Fallacies

1. *Is it true that too much farting can cause blindness or sterility?*
    NO! There is absolutely no scientific evidence to support this fallacy. It was probably created by parents who were afraid of their children abusing the fart.

2. *Do beans really warrant their reputation as a fart maker?*
    YES. Beans and other pulses (dried edible seeds) contain an antitryptic factor that interferes with the digestion of proteins. The undigested protein is worked on by bacteria to produce flatus. Fried foods also produce a lot of gas because they are so difficult to digest; a lot is left for the bacteria to work on.

3. *Does excitement enhance farting?*
    YES. Anything that speeds food through the digestive system (as excitement does) will create undigested food material reaching the colon, creating a feast for bacteria.

4. *Is it true that farts are flammable?*
    YES. As any college student can tell you the methane and hydrogen, if lit, will produce a gem-like flame.

5. *Is man at the top of the fart world?*

NO. Although well up on the scale of farters, man can't hold a candle to some of nature's farters. Man produces 400-1200 cc of flatus per day. A cow, whose diet is totally plant material, produces 300,000-600,000 cc. of gas per day. But the real gas guzzlers, ranking number one on the "toot meter", are the elephants, whose flatulance production runs into the millions of cc. per day.

6. *Is garlic a gas producer as well?*

NO. Garlic inhibits the growth of bacteria and therefore REDUCES the amount of flatus.

7. *Is it true that the extinction of the dinosaurs can be attributed to the fart?*

VERY POSSIBLE. The extinction of the dinosaur and the rise of the mammal coincide at about 70 million years ago, which has led scientists to the "furry fart theory".

With the mammals came the first true farts. The addition of extra methane and hydrogen sulfide to the air polluted the dinosaur's system and eventually came to interrupt the shell-forming glands of these reptiles. The soft eggs easily broke when jostled. With fewer eggs surviving, fewer and fewer dinosaurs survived until none were left.

8. *Is Gustav Andre Stool, the famous farting ventriloquist, still alive?*

YES. Now 83, the famous nightclub entertainer of the late 1940's, Stool presently resides in Miami Beach. During the late 40's and early 50's he amazed audiences around the country with his ability to throw a fart across the stage and into the audience. By the middle 50's his act ran out of steam. No longer in demand, he withdrew into seclusion. Surfacing again in the late 60's, full of bitterness, he secretly toured the country embarrassing dignitaries and show business types by throwing his farts at inopportune times. His final "performance" came at the second inauguration of Richard Nixon. Standing in the audience, some 100 feet from the stand, Stool threw his fart at Nixon right in the middle of the swearing in. At that moment the Chief Justice turned to a colleague and was heard to whisper, "An ominous air hovers over this administration".

Methane Mantra

4 cucumbers	½ cup bread crumbs
1 teaspoon salt	¼ cup wheat germ
¼ teaspoon pepper	1 egg lightly beaten

Skin cucumbers and cut into 1/3 inch slices. Dry between towels. Sprinkle with salt and pepper. Dip into crumbs and wheat germ, into egg and then into the crumbs and the wheat germ once more. Brown in butter (380°F). Drain in paper towels.

Fluff-o-Meter reading comes in at 4.3. This dish originated in Tibet centuries ago by Buddist monks who would try to create a perfect "OM" sound through their sphinctors. (Ahhhhh! Nirvana! Who stepped on the yak?)

Broccoli Belly Laugh

1 chopped onion	1 egg yolk
6 tablespoons butter	1 cup Parmesan cheese
4 tablespoons flour	2½ pounds cooked broccoli
2 cups milk	½ cup wheat germ
½ teaspoon salt	½ cup bread crumbs
¼ teaspoon pepper	

Cook onions in 4 tablespoons of butter till tender. Stir in flour and add milk gradually, stirring till it thickens. Add pepper, salt, egg yolk, and cheese. Pour half of sauce into greased pan. Arrange broccoli on top and cover with the rest of the sauce. Sprinkle with wheat germ and bread crumbs and dot with remaining butter. Bake in hot oven 400°F. about 20 minutes.

7.1 on Fluff-o-Meter. This dish has been the number one dish at the International Bacteria Yodeling Festival, three years in a row.

Swamp Gas Soup

1 cup apple juice

½ cup toasted soy beans

¼ cup toasted wheat germ

½ cup coconut

Heat apple juice to liking. Pour it into the mixture of other ingredients. Stir and serve.

A 4 on the Fluff meter. AHHHHH!! The fragrance of skunk cabbage now that spring is here! For conservative farters, but you'll still make the bull frogs green with envy. Mellow flatulence. (Known in the Everglades as "Gator Repellent")

Mount St. Helen's Cauliflower

1 head of cauliflower	¼ teaspoon pepper
½ cup of bread crumbs	2 eggs (beaten)
¼ cup of toasted wheat germ	4 tablespoons oil

Cook cauliflower in salt water for 10 minutes. Drain and cool. Separate into florets. Dip each piece into crumbs and wheat germ, then into eggs and back into crumbs and wheat germ again.

Heat oil in medium skillet. Fry florets until golden brown. Drain on paper towels. Serves 4 to 6.

A powerful dish. Look at that needle jump! Give it an 8 on the Fluff-o-Meter! Put the women and children in the storm cellars!

Royal Bean Royal

1 can of beans

½ cup of tofu (soy curd)

3 tablespoons of wheat germ

Mix ingredients in sauce pan and warm.

8.7 on the Fluff-o-Meter! Your bacteria will send you fan mail.

Chili Dogs (hot dogs with chili sauce)

Peanuts

Beer

7.9 on Fluff-o-Meter. Once caused quite a stir during a baseball game at Yankee Stadium. A batter hit the ball deep into the centerfield bleachers for a home run. However, as the ball sailed into the stands, the third base umpire came running towards the third base stands, yelling, "FOUL!, FOUL!". The players ran out onto the field in disbelief ready to argue until it was discovered that the umpire was yelling at my friends and I who had been dining on Stadium Stinkers and surpassing even the reliable Fluff meter. (At a football game we were called for unsportsmanlike conduct.)

Sunrise Serenade

1 cup sunflower seeds

½ cup wheat germ

½ cup puffed oats

4 pinches coconut

Talk to me Fluff-o-Meter! 7 sounds good.

This one's for those morning traffic jams. You won't have to use your horn. (Don't use if you car pool with your boss or anyone with respiratory problems.)

The True Colors of the Fart

To truly understand the nature of flatulence (the fart) we must remove it from its misty clouds of myth; disregard the heavy shroud of speculation which surrounds it. Farting is purely and simply a biological process that originates in the lower part of the digestive system. Each day an individual will produce anywhere from 400 to 1200 cc. of flatus. The quantity and quality is dependent upon diet to which we address ourselves in this book.

The first 10 feet or so of the intestine absorbs digested nutrition into the blood stream which will carry it to the cells. But . . . all nutrition cannot be absorbed, some will miss the boat. In the colon it will become fuel, cannon fodder, so to speak, created by that indispensible element in the fart, bacteria.

All throughout our lives these tiny, one celled plants reside in our colons. Here they feed upon our unused food stuffs and, in return, leave behind vitamin K, vitamin B_{12} and . . . FLATUS!

In breaking down the contents of a common fart we find the following:

NITROGEN	50%
CARBON DIOXIDE	40%
METHANE	
HYDROGEN	} 10%
HYDROGEN SULFIDE	

Each gas has its own story to tell. Each comes from a different source but, like a string quartet, they come together to make the music of the flatus.

NITROGEN makes up about 78% of the air we breathe. Some of the air we breathe misses the lungs and finds its way to the stomach. This is more apt to occur while we are eating. From the stomach these bubbles of nitrogen slowly find their way to the colon. The sound of the "stomach turning" is simply these nitrogen bubbles, mixed with air, rolling through the intestine to the promised land.

CARBON DIOXIDE comes from three possible sources: 1. It may enter the intestine from the blood. 2. It can result from the breakdown of sugars by the bacteria which have taken up residence in the colon and 3. Our intestines create bicarbonates to neutralize the acids that enter from the stomach. When bacteria breaks down the bicarbonates, carbon dioxide forms.

METHANE results from bacteria breaking down unabsorbed amino acids (the material of which proteins are made).

HYDROGEN also results from the breaking down of unabsorbed foods.

Neanderthal Bison Blaster

½ cup raw cashews

2 tablespoons wheat germ

½ cup coconut

¼ cup raisins

4 tablespoons pineapple juice

Mix ingredients. Sprinkle pineapple juice over mixture.

9.4 fluffer. Tops in this book! Your underwear may sneak out your zipper.

Thunder Wafers

1 banana

4 tablespoons of toasted wheat germ

3 tablespoons of coconut

6 diced raw cashews

Mix all the ingredients except the banana. Cut the banana into 8-12 coin like

sections. Roll the banana sections into the mixture so the entire piece is covered.

Be sure ample amount of cashews get lodged into each section.

Rates a 7.5 on the Fluff-o-Meter. Strong thrust has been known to lift a person from their seat. Potent propulsion. For "macho farters" only. If you value your friends, restrict intake of Thunder Wafers to 5 per sitting. If banana sections are placed between two slices of wheat bread it's known as the "Sonic Boom Sandwich".

½ onion (chopped)

¼ cup butter

1 tablespoon curry powder

½ cup water

¼ cup lentils (cooked)

¼ cup peas

2 cups rice

½ tablespoon salt

1 tablespoon lemon juice

Saute onion in butter till lightly brown. Add curry, water, salt and lemon juice.
Cook lentils, rice and peas. Mix together.

Lucky 7 on Fluff. Good old Gunga Din wouldn't have needed his trumpet to signal the British regiment if he had eaten this dish.

1 cup wheat germ

1 cup granola

raisins (To your liking. Be generous.)

1 cup cold milk

Rates an 8. Starts your day off with a bang! (Talk about snap, crackle, pop!)

Available at fine book stores everywhere or order direct from the publisher by

DOUBLE EAGLE, INC.

1124 N. Derbyshire
Arlington Hts., IL 60004

THE I LOVE TO **Fart** COOKBOOK

To order one copy simply enclose $4.95 plus $1.25 shipping and handling. For order of 5 or more copies, publisher pays all mailing and handling charge.

Illinois residents add 5% state sales tax.

Enclosed is $ _____ plus $ _____ shipping and handling.

Please send _____ copies.

Mailing Label — Please print clearly

_____
Name
_____
Address
_____
City   State   Zip